D1558509

PRIVACY and SOCIAL MEDIA

CONTEMPORARY ISSUES

CRIMINAL JUSTICE SYSTEM
EDUCATION
THE ENVIRONMENT
GENDER EQUALITY
GUN CONTROL
HEALTH CARE
IMMIGRATION
JOBS AND ECONOMY
MENTAL HEALTH
POVERTY AND WELFARE
PRIVACY AND SOCIAL MEDIA
RACE RELATIONS
RELIGIOUS FREEDOM

PRIVACY and SOCIAL MEDIA

ASHLEY NICOLE

MASON CREST
PHILADELPHIA | MIAMI

MASON CREST

450 Parkway Drive, Suite D, Broomall, Pennsylvania 19008
(866) MCP-BOOK (toll-free) • www.masoncrest.com

© 2020 by Mason Crest, an imprint of National Highlights, Inc.

Printed and bound in the United States of America.

CPSIA Compliance Information: Batch #CCRI2019.
For further information, contact Mason Crest at 1-866-MCP-Book.

First printing
1 3 5 7 9 8 6 4 2

ISBN (hardback) 978-1-4222-4399-2
ISBN (series) 978-1-4222-4387-9
ISBN (ebook) 978-1-4222-7414-9

Library of Congress Cataloging-in-Publication Data
on file at the Library of Congress

Interior and cover design: Torque Advertising + Design
Production: Michelle Luke

QR CODES AND LINKS TO THIRD-PARTY CONTENT

CONTENTS

KEY ICONS TO LOOK FOR:

 Words to Understand: These words with their easy-to-understand definitions will increase the reader's understanding of the text while building vocabulary skills.

 Sidebars: This boxed material within the main text allows readers to build knowledge, gain insights, explore possibilities, and broaden their perspectives by weaving together additional information to provide realistic and holistic perspectives.

 Educational videos: Readers can view videos by scanning our QR codes, providing them with additional educational content to supplement the text. Examples include news coverage, moments in history, speeches, iconic sports moments, and much more!

 Text-Dependent Questions: These questions send the reader back to the text for more careful attention to the evidence presented there.

 Research Projects: Readers are pointed toward areas of further inquiry connected to each chapter. Suggestions are provided for projects that encourage deeper research and analysis.

 Series Glossary of Key Terms: This back-of-the-book glossary contains terminology used throughout this series. Words found here increase the reader's ability to read and comprehend higher-level books and articles in this field.

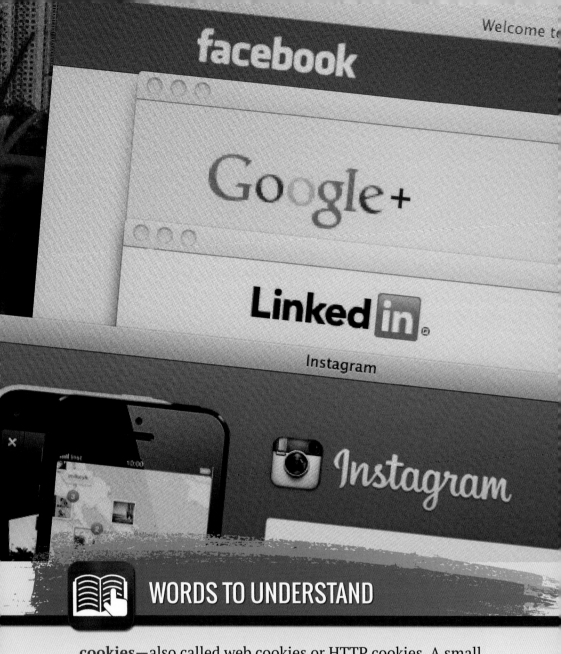

WORDS TO UNDERSTAND

cookies—also called web cookies or HTTP cookies. A small piece of data stored on a user's computer by a web browser from a particular website.

engagement—participation or involvement.

viral—relating to an image, video, piece of information, or other type of media that is spread rapidly and widely from one person to another.

OVERVIEW OF SOCIAL MEDIA AND PRIVACY

Today, an estimated 2.8 billion people around the world are using social media. Most of these people use networks like Facebook, YouTube, WhatsApp, Instagram, or WeChat. Each year, new social media websites and apps roll out, presenting new opportunities to engage with friends, family members, and even strangers.

Most Americans probably have some experience using one of the most popular social media websites. But a question remains: what exactly is social media?

Generally speaking, social media facilitate the creation and sharing of information and ideas online. Social media websites include virtual communities and networks that revolve around user-generated content, including text posts, videos, and photos. These websites offer connection to other individuals via electronic devices: smart phones, laptops, personal computers, or tablets.

The role of social media in the daily lives of Americans remains controversial. Its prominence in today's society brings up many questions. In order to answer some of them, it is helpful to examine the rich history of the web and the resources created over this medium in the last few decades.

THE HISTORY OF SOCIAL MEDIA

Many people think social media got its start in the early 2000s with the rise of sites like Myspace. The truth is that forms of social media have a rich history, with roots extending earlier than the advent of the computer. Understanding social media's history can help to better predict its future.

The telegraph, invented in the 1840s, was a precursor to social media. The invention established one of the first ways to connect people throughout the country electronically, without the need to mail a letter. The telegraph worked by transmitting electrical signals over wires connecting stations to each other. The device's inventor, Samuel Morse, created a code that assigned meaning to the electronic signals. His invention was improved upon in the 1870s, with the invention of the telephone. These developments showed that technology would lead to other forms of long-distance communication in the future.

A major step toward the development of social media occurred in the late 1960s, with the creation of ARPANET. Computers had been invented during the 1940s, to help in the American effort during World War II. They were improved upon during the 1950s and 1960s, but at the time were so large that only major businesses, research universities, and government agencies owned them. In 1969, the US Advanced Research Projects Agency connected computers at four universities, creating the first network. The computers could "talk" to each other, enabling researchers to share data and work together. Essentially, ARPANET was the basis for the modern Internet that people use today. Over time, more computers were connected to ARPANET, and communication exchange via computing progressed throughout the 1970s.

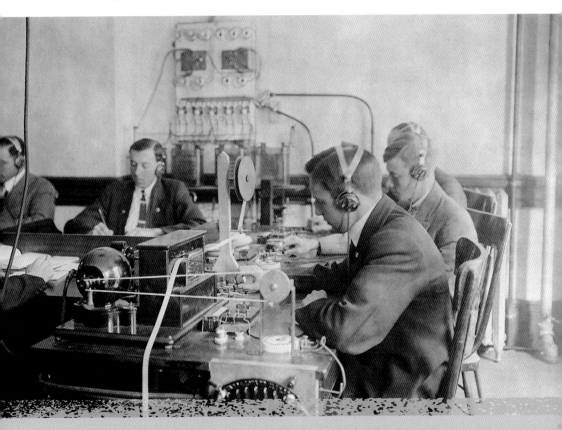

Students practice sending Morse Code messages using a telegraph key at the Marconi training school in New York, 1912.

ARPANET, the forerunner of the modern Internet, was created so that large mainframe computers used by the US military and by universities and research organizations could easily share data.

In fact, forum applications and instant messaging existed as early as 1973.

Email and instant messages allow one-on-one communication. People could communicate with larger groups of the public through electronic bulletin boards, which today are often called message boards. Any computer user who logged in to a bulletin board could read messages posted by others, and respond to them. Initially, these boards were mostly text-based, hobbyist-run services. The first electronic bulletin board, Community

Memory, came to fruition in 1973, followed by Usenet in 1979. Soon enough, most of the country's major cities had their own bulletin board systems for personal computer users. Most bulletin boards were used to chat or trade, but some were set up as online text-based games.

As more people began to use personal computers and connect to the Internet in the 1990s, social networking sites began to develop. Some of the early ones were GeoCities and Classmates. Another was called Six Degrees, and allowed users to register and connect with friends. Users could send messages and share posts with those in their inner circles. Though Six Degrees was short-lived, lasting from 1997 to 2000, it was a precursor for modern social networking programs.

As the 2000s began, web users became entranced by

English computer scientist Timothy Berners-Lee invented the World Wide Web in 1989.

Live Journal, Open Diary, Myspace, Friendster, LinkedIn, and Facebook. Blogging also became increasingly popular. Soon, people were becoming used to sharing their photos, thoughts, and videos on the Internet with their friends.

TYPES OF SOCIAL MEDIA

Today, several types of social media exist. They typically offer different benefits. First are networks used to facilitate social connections. These include apps that allow you to communicate with friends and family members, like Facebook or Twitter. Some of these websites facilitate making new friends as well.

Next, there are apps designed for sharing multimedia content, like photos and videos. Multimedia social media apps include YouTube and Instagram. Users can view content and often "like" or comment on it, just as they can on Facebook. Users also have the option of sharing with friends or to a larger audience.

Some social media apps are designed for professional networking, to help adults make connections that will boost their careers. For example, LinkedIn offers opportunities to connect with potential employers, post resumes, and search for employment.

Finally, some social media sites are designed with the intent of spreading information. They are information or educational. For instance, you might find a website that is designed to help people complete their home improvement projects or learn about building cars.

Every minute, more than 100 hours of video are uploaded to YouTube. The app was created in 2005, and today has more than a billion users.

No matter how people use social media, paying attention to privacy concerns and other issues is important. Users should always assume that any information they post online will always be there for others to see.

GOING VIRAL

When people talk about videos that have become incredibly popular, they often say that they have "gone **viral**." Viral content spreads quickly over social networks, not unlike a physical virus that causes an epidemic of illness.

Viral content consists of material that is likely to be shared among social networks. Today, many websites offer easy ways to spread content among friends. For example, Twitter offers a "retweet" button, Pinterest allows you to

 CONSEQUENCES OF SOCIAL MEDIA POSTS

Can people get into trouble for social media posts? Apart from the social implications of posting certain information online, a user may also face professional, civil, and criminal consequences, depending on what is posted.

Seventeen states, including California, Arkansas, Illinois, and Washington, have passed laws that protecting employees from being forced to share the usernames and passwords associated with their social media accounts with their employers. However, these laws do not prevent employers from firing their employees if they make inappropriate social media posts. For example, an employee who reveals confidential information about his or her company on Facebook or Instagram could be filed. An employee can also be filed for sharing offensive memes, particularly if the poster can be identified as an employee of the "pin" websites, and Facebook lets you share posts with friends at the click of a button. Social media websites thrive on their users making content go viral through these sharing methods.

Businesses often utilize viral marketing as a way of spreading advertisements in a way that is not obvious. Some businesses may pay for content that will appeal to a wide variety of customers. Sometimes businesses are able to create content so compelling that they do not even need to pay to air it—social media users will distribute the

company. An employee could even be fired for using work computers to search for a new employer.

For students, college or trade school admissions could also be impacted by social media posts. School administrators do use Google to learn more about applicants. Those who post offensive jokes or comments, or photos depicting alcohol or drug use, might have trouble getting into the school they want.

Social media posts may count as admissible evidence in a legal case. A parent who seeks custody of children may fail to receive custody rights if there are photos on social media showing the parent using illegal drugs. Posts have also affected legal cases involving criminal charges and insurance fraud.

Social media use can have extensive consequences for users of all ages. The actions people take on the Internet can have very real-life effects.

In 2017, US intelligence agency officials reported that foreign companies and governments had used social networks and online services in an effort to influence millions of Americans before the 2016 presidential election. Robert Mueller was appointed to investigate alleged collaboration between the presidential campaign of Donald Trump and the Russian government.

content for them. This makes social media an affordable form of advertisement for major corporations. In the past, viral marketing has worked for everything from promoting television shows and books to selling items like fidget spinners and drones.

Viral advertising makes sense for many companies. Not only is it affordable, but this marketing method also offers a large potential reach. In a time when many people forgo cable or forward through commercials, even big corporations are looking for a better way to reach the average web user. Additionally, viral marketing does build up a brand's personality.

One way companies can increase viewership for their advertisements is through the use of Internet "bots"—automated programs that mimic the natural interactions of humans. Bots can comment, follow other users, and share material to "friends."

Concern over the use of bots became more widespread after the 2016 presidential election, as Americans learned how these programs were used to spread false material about the candidates to voters in an attempt to influence the election. The material that bots spread blends in well with other viral content, making it different for even savvy web users to tell the difference.

Using bots is a controversial method for advertising. In fact, the use of bots has led to recent discussions involving fraud. Because laws are not always able to keep up with technology, it could be years before the world sees changes to laws regarding the way companies and organizations use advertising bots.

BENEFITS AND DRAWBACKS OF SOCIAL MEDIA USE

Social media is not without its benefits. If social media did not offer benefit, it would not have billions of users around the world. Among the biggest benefits of social media is the improved sense of connection it creates to the outside world, including real and online communities. When you use social media, you might be building relationships that last years, perhaps even the rest of your life. You might be talking to somebody in another country or perhaps another language. You would not have this experience without the help of social media. This explains why people of all generations are increasingly using social media.

Social media **engagement** plays a significant role in the ability of organizations and groups to garner attention. Group organizers hope that fellow social media users will feel compelled to respond to comments, post pictures, and perhaps eventually participate in real-life events. Without social media marketing, would advocacy groups around the world have such a strong voice? Raising awareness is a major goal social media can help accomplish.

Of course, it is also important to pay attention to the potential drawbacks of social media. For example, corporations often use social media as a marketing technique. You might think you are having a genuine interaction with somebody, but you might begin to realize this individual or organization is only reaching out to you with the intention of selling you something. This has been the case for many people who found themselves interacting with bots used for advertising and political purposes.

Additionally, it is notable how many issues arise as a result of heavy social media use. Depression, cyberbullying, and harassment exist among social media users. These are issues this book is going to delve deeper into, as their impact cannot be ignored.

EXPLORING INTERNET PRIVACY

Internet privacy is an increasingly important issue as users became more inclined to share their personal information with social media websites and online friends. The information you share on the web can reveal more than you might think. A photo you post in front of your house may reveal your home address, the car you drive, or even what kind of security your home offers. It is wise to pay attention to what you reveal to the public through social media.

Approximately 7 million Americans are victims of identity theft each year. Information shared on social media can give hackers clues that can help them access a person's bank account.

On the other hand, there are some ways in which you transmit information about yourself on the Internet without even knowing it. You might be revealing information about your Internet use and habits merely by visiting some of your favorite websites.

Many people do not realize that social media websites often store, repurpose, and provide to third parties the information provided by its users. Much of the data these websites need is stored on your computer through **cookies**. You use these cookies to automate access to your most frequented websites. While cookies can be advantageous to your web usage, some companies will use cookies to get more information about your habits on the Internet. This enables them to target advertisements based on things that you have searched for in the recent past.

Netscape invented the cookie in 1994. The goal was to

Scan here to see Mark Zuckerberg speak about Internet privacy.

We didn't take a broad enough view of our responsibility

0:00 | 0:00

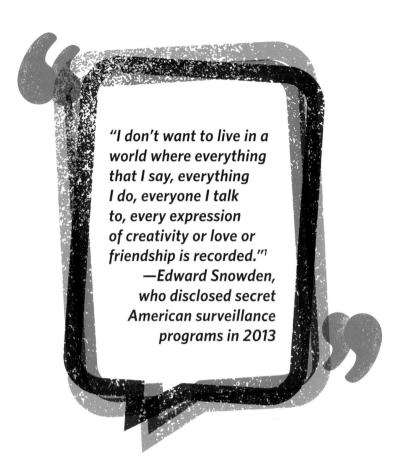

"I don't want to live in a world where everything that I say, everything I do, everyone I talk to, every expression of creativity or love or friendship is recorded."[1]
—Edward Snowden, who disclosed secret American surveillance programs in 2013

track the behavior of web users to make recommendations and better advertise to them based on their specific interests. Cookies can also track preferences so that the website can make adjustments when an individual visits.

"For the most part, Americans haven't loudly objected to this slow erosion of privacy: Much of our personal information has been surrendered willingly as a result of our eagerness to connect through social media and our ravenous consumption habits," writes Charles Mahtesian for National Public Radio. "What many consumers don't know, however, is how aggressively Big Tech has moved to track and combine the data to build user profiles."[2]

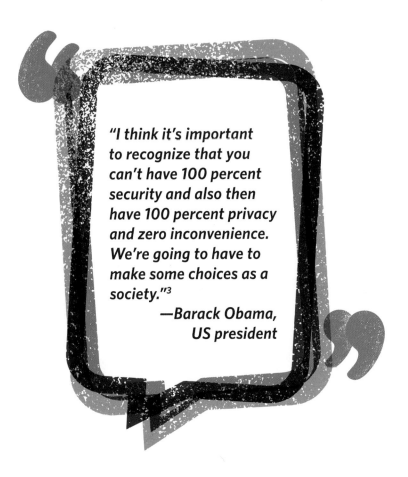

"I think it's important to recognize that you can't have 100 percent security and also then have 100 percent privacy and zero inconvenience. We're going to have to make some choices as a society."[3]

—Barack Obama, US president

In 1995, the European Union passed its first laws protecting privacy on the Internet. By 1997, America also had growing concerns regarding privacy. The Electronic Privacy Information Center reviewed the most popular websites at the time and found that only 17 of 100 had privacy policies. Of those privacy policies, none met the basic standards.

In 1997, President Bill Clinton created the Information Infrastructure Task Force, which defined information privacy as "an individual's claim to control the terms under which personal information ... is acquired, disclosed, and used."[4] The Internet was still developing at the time, and many of the privacy issues American face today were not as significant in the 1990s. For example, social media websites were not as widely used.

In the aftermath of the World Trade Center attacks on September 11, 2001, President Bush signed the Patriot Act into law. This legislation gave federal intelligence agencies and law-enforcement organizations more power to find and track potential terrorists through surveillance of electronic communications.

In 2006, Facebook released a new feature called News Feed. On the feed, people could see changes their friends made to their profiles. Many Facebook users disapproved of this option because it showcased some of the more private changes, like those related to relationship status, to the rest of the world. When web users complained the feature was invasive, Facebook allowed users to opt for greater privacy control.

Just a few years later, in 2009, Facebook changed its privacy policies again. As a result, anything posted to Facebook could be used by the company in any way it wanted. Even material that had been uploaded to the app by people who later wanted to quit and deleted their accounts was up for grabs. Again, the public was displeased, and Facebook opted to revise this policy.

Facebook came under fire once again in 2018 when the public learned that the app had enabled the collection of personal data from 87 million users by a political consulting firm, Cambridge Analytica. The company had acquired the Facebook data to target voters, prompting questions about the way Facebook collects and sells its users' information. Facebook founder Mark Zuckerberg was required to testify in front of Congress regarding the matter.

Information posted online, including addresses, phone numbers, or the place where people work or go to school, could be accessed by any individual or corporation. This information could put people at risk for a malicious attack. The posting of photos on the Internet has become especially controversial in recent years. Many people are unwillingly tagged on social media sites. Whether someone wants to be posted on the Internet or not, their identity could be identified and exposed through developing facial recognition technology.

Another privacy issue has arisen with the likes of Google Street View, which was released in 2007. Many people objected to photos of their homes being placed on the website for all to view. While the website did opt to blur information like license plates, questions remain regarding the privacy issues of the feature.

Privacy issues are nowhere near resolved in the United States, and social media only brings about more questions. Understanding the impact of the Internet and electronic communication on privacy is critical to understanding the development of new regulations for the industry.

TEXT-DEPENDENT QUESTIONS

1. What were three of the first social media websites?
2. Name two presidents who passed legislation linked to privacy issues in the United States.
3. What is one potential consequence of social media use? What is one benefit?
4. What invention may have been the first precursor for the Internet?

 RESEARCH PROJECTS

Choose one of the first social media sites leading up to the advent of Facebook. Research its history. Who founded the website, and for what reason? What features did the social media site offer? What kind of privacy policy did the website offer? Create a presentation answering these questions and discussing some of the related privacy issues.

WORDS TO UNDERSTAND

adolescence—the period of time between the onset of puberty and development into an adult.

cyberbullying—the use of electronic communication to bully somebody. Often pursued through threats, intimidation, and name-calling.

consensus—a general or overall agreement.

neurotransmitters—chemical substances released at the ends of nerve fibers, like chemical signals.

DOES SOCIAL MEDIA BENEFIT ADOLESCENTS?

CHAPTER 2

Many struggles come with **adolescence**, making this period of time particularly difficult for teens who use social media. This period of time is one in which teens are trying to determine who they are, and there is often a discrepancy between appearances and reality. Social media allows its users to create an online image not representative of reality.

Statistics suggest that more than half of American teenagers use Facebook, while more teens use other websites like YouTube and Instagram. In spite of the fact that so many young people use social media today, researchers still struggle to find a **consensus** about the effects of social media.

Smartphones have played a significant role in getting teens to use social media. Most teenagers surveyed by the Pew Research Center in 2018 had access to a smartphone. About 45 percent of teenagers reported to Pew that they are online almost constantly.[5]

Most teenagers surveyed by the Pew Research Center reported that social media had a positive impact on their lives. Teenagers expressed the ability to connect with others, including family members and friends. Some teenagers also expressed the ability to have more access to information and news. The positive impact they reported on entertainment, self-expression, and social support were also notable.

CYBERBULLYING

Cyberbullying is another issue adults consider when they think about whether their children should be involved with social media. Cyberbullying creates an imbalance of power between adolescents with the help of the Internet. Sometimes cyberbullying may seem merely annoying and benign, but other times it can feel ominous and threatening. Cyberbullying often consists of the posting of private communications to the public, spreading rumors, or being aggressive.

One way people cyberbully others is through a technique called "trolling." Trolling often involves harassing and inflaming others on the web either to elicit a strong reaction or for personal amusement.

One study suggests that up to 40 percent of adolescents may have been victims of cyberbullying.[6] Additionally, researchers know that girls are more likely to become targets of cyberbullying than boys are. Additionally, teens who have a more active web presence are more likely to become targets compared to teens who do not have active social media profiles.[7]

Of course, the impact is not all positive. Some teenagers reported negative effects on their age group from social media. The negative implications include increased bullying and increased spread of rumors and gossip. Teens expressed feeling that social media platforms could harm relationships or lead to less meaningful interactions between people. Additionally, teens reported that social media created an unrealistic depiction of life.

Cyberbullying does have negative consequences, including anxiety, depression, and decreased self-esteem. The physical impacts may be surprising too. They include insomnia, bed-wetting, fatigue, and stomach ailments. Victims of cyberbullying are also at higher risk for low test scores and low grades.[8] They are also at increased risk for violent behavior, suicidal behavior, and increased substance abuse.

Students report that bullying is more likely to happen offline than online. In fact, 67 percent of teens surveyed reported that offline harassment was much more common than cyberbullying.[9]

Thanks to high-profile cases in the news, cyberbullying is becoming a more prominent issue in the media. Shedding light on cyberbullying has encouraged schools, parents, and other organizations to take action. While some controversy currently exists regarding how far schools should go to punish cyberbullying that happens off campus, most schools now have their own policies regarding Internet conduct.

A recent policy statement by the American Academy of Pediatrics (AAP), notes,

> The AAP has delineated its concerns about media violence, sex in the media, substance use, music and music videos, obesity and the media, and infant media use. At the same time, existing AAP policy discusses the positive, prosocial uses of media and the need for media education in schools and at home. Shows like "Sesame Street" can help children learn numbers and letters, and the media can also teach empathy, racial and ethnic tolerance, and a whole variety of interpersonal skills. Prosocial media may also influence teenagers. Helping behaviors can increase after listening to prosocial (rather than neutral) song lyrics, and positive information about adolescent health is increasingly available through new media, including YouTube videos and campaigns that incorporate cell phone text messages.[10]

The following essays will address whether or not social media benefits adolescents. Read the two opposing viewpoints to understand the potential consequences and benefits for teenagers who use social media.

To learn more about cyberbullying, scan here.

SOCIAL MEDIA PROVIDES BENEFITS FOR ADOLESCENTS

Teenagers who have expressed the benefits they experience from social media may have a point. After all, social media can provide valuable connections to the outside world. This essay will explore the benefits of social media for adolescents. Those who benefit from social media may be able to demonstrate the advantages they have gained through the web.

Social media provides a beneficial connection to the outside world in addition to family members and friends. No longer do friendships and relationships have to end because somebody has moved far away. Family members who live on different continents can stay in touch. In fact, social media may offer the advantage of strengthening some relationships.

For some people, social media aids communication with others by providing a medium through which they can express themselves. When words fail to convey a message, some people might prefer to send a message via social media. This provides an easy way to stay in touch rather than allowing relationships to fall to the wayside.

Additionally, children are less likely to experience feelings like isolation and detriments of cyberbullying when they also have the opportunity to develop friendships.[11] For some adolescents, offline relationships can flourish with the help of social media. Children who lack some social skills may learn appropriate interactions by talking with friends over text or instant messaging systems.

Social media use also improves the ability of teenagers to use technology. Information technology is a significant force in improved quality of life and economic growth. Building a future workforce consisting of adolescents who understand technology may improve the country's prospects for education, healthcare, energy, security, and other industries.

Researchers also believe social media use may improve creativity of adolescents. Sharing art, music, writing, and other creative endeavors with both acquaintances and strangers has never been easier than on the Internet. Adolescents can also develop their ideas through new creative media, like podcasts and blogs.

In addition to boosting creativity, social media may also lead to an increase in critical thinking and problem-solving skills. When adolescents read social media posts, they often compare their own values to others. They may also benefit from the exposure to other ways of thinking. In a way, social media use may also work as an exploration into different schools of thought. Additionally, reading social media posts also means students may have to find new ways to support their own opinions after the post online.

Could it be that social media use even encourages discourse and improved social skills teens and young adults? Teenagers who engage with their peers online while also maintaining strong in-person social engagement can actually reap benefits from the web. Plus, being involved with social groups online creates a sense of inclusion and emotional support. Teenagers feel accepted and loved by their peers when they have more people to engage with regularly.

In addition to social engagement, social media also offers advantages associated with altruism and volunteering. In fact, social media has been used to raise funding for large-

Social media can be a tool for young people to channel their creativity and express themselves. Whether their talent involves sports, music, writing, art, or technology, they can share it online and receive feedback and reinforcement. Studies show that allowing young people to express themselves builds self-confidence and increases happiness.

Young people use social media for more than just selfies. Some teens make YouTube videos or develop Twitter campaigns devoted to informing others about important issues in their communities and around the world. Using social media as a tool to affect the world can help young people to develop empathy, kindness, and gratitude.

scale projects important to the community. Adolescents can take part in these activities as well.

In the past, some have argued that social media use may have detrimental effects on children ages 9 and 10 who participate on websites like Instagram or who text. The truth is that some researchers found social media use was more commonly associated with less family conflict and fewer sleeping issues. It was actually higher use of

"While it is important for parents to instill healthy habits surrounding social media use, including limiting and monitoring time online, it is also important to recognize that social media is not a bad thing. It only becomes a bad thing when people misuse it for bullying, public shaming, and rumor spreading. In fact, research shows there are numerous benefits to social media use. "[12]
—*Sheri Gordon, author and bullying prevention expert*

general media, like television, Internet, and video games, that were detrimental to the family unit and sleep.

"The most important thing is that not all screen media is bad, if you want to put it in a nutshell," comments Dr. Martin Paulus, the scientific director at the Laureate Institute for Brain Research in Tulsa, Oklahoma. "There's a lot of pre-existing biases that if we expose kids to media, something terrible is going to happen. What we show is that's not the case."[13]

Finally, it is important to acknowledge the benefits of adolescents having increased access to information. For example, minors now have increased access to information about health and safety. Mobile technology may improve adherence to medication, access to healthcare appointments, and access to information that helps young people make healthcare decisions.

Additionally, teenagers benefit from the ability to learn new skills online. Social media offers an easy way to share videos like those that can teach people how to do things like play guitar, cook lasagna, or perform a skateboarding trick. Watching videos on the web offers new insights to potential hobbies and skills. This is a more affordable way to learn skills than taking a formal class.

There are many things parents can do to help their children benefit from social media. Taking an active role in overseeing what their children are doing on the web is critical. For instance, parents may decide that their children are not viewing offensive material or receiving threatening messages from their peers. Parents can facilitate a positive relationship between their child and the web.

In assessing the many benefits of using social media, it is easy to see why so many teenagers thrive in an area of widely available media. This is not to say that all social media is perfect, but it is not fair to throw away potential benefits because of a few drawbacks.

SOCIAL MEDIA DOES NOT BENEFIT ADOLESCENTS

Many experts feel that social media has detrimental effects on adolescents. Adolescence is a time of significant developmental change. Additionally, this period of time often comes with limited capacity for self-regulation and increased opportunity to fall to peer pressure. Adolescents are also prone to experimentation with everything from new styles to new substances.

For example, social media may subject children to risk-taking behaviors. Researchers have found a link connecting both sexting and cyberbullying to increased

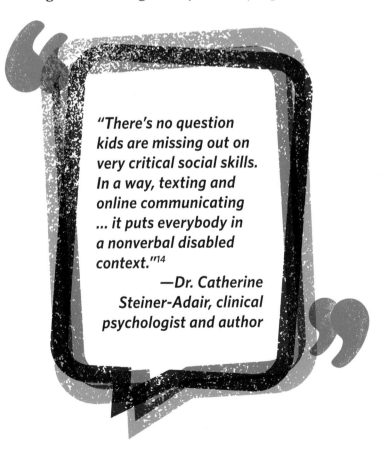

"There's no question kids are missing out on very critical social skills. In a way, texting and online communicating ... it puts everybody in a nonverbal disabled context."[14]

—*Dr. Catherine Steiner-Adair, clinical psychologist and author* risk of pregnancy and sexually transmitted infections.[15] For this reason, many parents caution their children from using social media. Some parents also use content filters to ensure that their children only have access to the websites they approve of their child visiting.

Social media can also introduce pornography to minors, even if they are not seeking it out. Approximately 70 percent of adolescents between the ages of fifteen and seventeen have reported accidental exposure to pornography according to one study.[16] Exposure to

Cyberstalking is a form of cyberbullying that generally involves a person who follows one specific person through their social media platforms to harass or threaten them.

pornography is linked to risk-taking behaviors and changing attitudes toward relationships and women.

In the same vein, sexualized text communications, also known sexting, is a trend growing among adolescents as well. The detrimental effects for young people who communicate in this way include potential public release of sexual images and messages. In addition to public shaming and embarrassment, the release of these materials could also impact future job and education prospects.

Sexting images of minors is also a legal issue in the criminal court system. Anybody who is accused of taking or disseminating photos depicting minors in sexual situations is subject to child pornography charges. Even minors who spread photos of other minors may be charged with possession of child pornography. The consequences can follow these minors for the rest of their lives.

Internet addiction is another detrimental component of social media use. Addiction to the Internet occurs when somebody uses it uncontrollably or in excess to the point that it causes social dysfunction. Internet addiction works similarly to other forms of addiction in that it can cause interpersonal problems and even physical issues. In fact, people who experience addiction to the web may also experience depression, self-harm, increased alcohol use, and extreme weight gain.[17] Additionally, studies have found a link between addiction to the Internet and a decrease in the volume of gray matter in the brain. It also impacts the brain's chemicals, or **neurotransmitters**.

Electronic media may have something to do with sleeping disturbances in adolescents. Children who get fewer than six hours of sleep may report higher incidences of depression, suicidal thoughts, and poor academic performance. Electronic devices contribute to disruption of the body's circadian rhythm because of the light they emit. With about 60 percent of adolescents using their phones in the last hour before they go to sleep, they are getting less sleep and less quality sleep than those who do not use their phones. "Lack of sleep in adolescents has been associated with lack of productivity, depression, lack of energy, and poor school performance," write the authors of a 2017 study published in the journal *Global Pediatric Health*. "Studies have established a foundation of declining sleep quality and quantity in adolescents that partake in texting at bedtime or even after 'lights out.'"[18]

Mental health issues may also have a link to social media use. A 2017 study demonstrated that the rates of depressive symptoms increased by about 33 percent in a span of five years (2010 to 2015). During this time period, the rate of suicide for teenage girls also increased by 65 percent. The mental health link to social media could have roots in decreased self-esteem and cyberbullying issues. "Changes in social interaction are especially relevant for suicide and suicide-related outcomes," write the authors of a 2017 study published in the journal *Clinical Psychological Science*. "Given the recent shifts in adolescent social interaction, increases in both perceived burdensomeness

A 2018 study found that 15 percent of teens say that have sent a naked photo of themselves to someone else, and 27 percent of teens say they have received a sext. However, many young people don't understand that there can be legal consequences to sexting.

[for example, feeling as though one is a burden on others] and thwarted belongingness [feelings of loneliness and alienation] may be particularly salient risk factors for suicide in this population."[19]

Many parents worry about the digital footprint their children may leave behind. A digital footprint consists of any information or data a person has left on the web. This information could include every website a person has visited, all videos they have posted, and any updates they have made to a social media profile. Some of the information adolescents post online may have long-lasting implications. Universities and employers look at this information before making admissions and hiring decisions.

Speaking of a digital footprint, this brings up privacy concerns for social media users as well. Technology has made it difficult for even teenage web users to hide. Personal information about individuals, even minors, can be found on the Internet.

Some people even use fake identities in an attempt to hide from other web users. Using a fake identity on social media to trick somebody is known as "catfishing." Some people use fake identities to meet with potential suitors on dating websites or as an attempt to increase their self-esteem on social media.

Finally, many adults worry that younger generations may lose out on essential social skills. The notion of future adults hiding behind their screens may be worrying. Parents may worry that their children will struggle to make friends as they grow up because they are so used to talking to friends on the phone.

Ultimately, it is clear that social media does have some detrimental effects on children and adolescents. While many people enjoy social media, studies show that its use does come with some negative consequences. Some researchers may advise against allowing children to use these platforms in spite of any potential benefits they offer.

TEXT-DEPENDENT QUESTIONS

1. Are boys or girls more likely to become victims of cyberbullying?
2. What is a digital footprint?
3. How does social media use impact sleep?
4. How might access to social media and the web impact healthcare?

RESEARCH PROJECTS

Choose one benefit or consequence associated with social media to research. Create a hypothesis based on this characteristic. For instance, you might hypothesize that social media has a negative impact on teenage self-esteem. Find at least three research studies that support or contradict your hypothesis and write about how they shape your view of social media. Does Social Media Benefit Adolescents?

socioeconomic status—a measure of an individual's work experience, economic position, social position, income, education, and employment.

demographics—data or statistics related to a specific population or group.

stratified—classified, categorized, or arranged.

DO TARGETED ADVERTISEMENTS BENEFIT INTERNET USERS?

CHAPTER 3

In the past, advertising was often done on billboards, in newspapers, and on the radio. Today, people view the bulk of advertising on the Internet. Online channels have made it easier for advertisers to reach wide audiences with less effort thanks to data-mining and web cookies.

In recent years, much Internet marketing has taken the form of targeted advertisements.

Targeted advertising is a form of marketing in which online firms can identify the audience that their research indicates will be most receptive. Companies examines certain **demographics** of their customers, including their race or ethnicity, **socioeconomic status**, gender, education, income level, and age, to determine who is most likely to purchase their product. Advertisements are also targeted based on a user's Internet browsing history, or their past online purchases. Companies tend to prefer targeted advertisements because it prevents them from wasting time advertising to people who are probably not interested in their products.

Most people have seen targeted ads, though they may not have noticed them. When people check their email, they may notice a banner advertisement at the top of the page. Other times people see advertisements listed on the side of a page of search results. These advertisements change, depending on the computer, phone, or device that is being used to view the web page. Cookies that have tracked the user's preferences and browsing history enable advertisements to appear in those places for things that the user had previously searched for or showed an online interest in.

It is obvious why advertisers prefer targeted advertisements to the older, more generic forms. For example, targeted advertising is much more affordable than trying to appeal to all consumers with one ad. With

Scan here to learn more about what Internet advertisers know about you.

Facebook ads

Facebook allows companies to target advertisements using general characteristics drawn from user profiles, such as gender, age, or location. More specific ads can be based on the social media user's online behavior and interests, as determined through searches.

reduced costs also comes minimal waste and a higher return on investment. Essentially, targeted advertisements take the guesswork out of marketing to consumers. Now, marketing firms have narrowed down the most concise ways to make statements to shoppers.

Public opinions are divided on the issue of targeted advertising. A 2012 Pew Research Center study found that 68 percent of Americans did not like the idea of their personal data being used for targeted advertising. More recent studies, including one conducted by the Annenberg School of Communications at the University

SOCIAL MEDIA MARKETING

Some marketing is specifically targeted toward users on social media. These ads differ somewhat from search engine marketing tactics based on how ads are created and how companies use data. Social media marketing targets the social media websites like Facebook and YouTube rather than Google or Bing.

One method advertisers use to target social media users is geotargeting, which helps advertisers pinpoint specific locations where they would like to advertise. Social media marketing also revolves around behavioral targeting based on material users add to their profiles. For instance, somebody who reports he is married and lives in Florida is going to see different advertisements than a single man who lives in Hawaii.

Additionally, the pages a user likes or follows on social media will impact advertisements as well. For example, a woman who follows many clothing brands on Facebook will see more clothing ads than a woman who follows mostly video game-related pages. These advertisements work so well because they rely on of Pennsylvania in 2016, indicate that many Americans have become resigned to the fact that their habits are being tracked for commercial use, but they do not like the practice or believe that it is fair. Younger Internet users and individuals who live in lower-income households tend to have a more favorable view of targeted ads, but even then the statistics are not generally favorable. Most view

repetition and sharing. You might think of social media marketing as "word of mouth" for the Internet.

Essentially, having a social media profile with any information on it provides information to advertisers. Facebook allows companies to use its data to target the people it wants to market products too. This creates the most effective method of advertisement for the web.

Two types of social media marketing exist: passive and active. An example of passive marketing is a company's social media profile collecting positive reviews that other consumers will see before making a decision to buy something. Active marketing on the web occurs when a company posts advertisements with the intention of reaching out to new consumers. Most experts consider a combination of the two techniques to be most effective.

Today, social media marketing makes up a significant portion of marketing for online and offline businesses. As a result, consumers are not likely to see a decline in this form of marketing in the near future.

Google AdWords

Overview   Benefits   How it works   Costs   Testimonials   Get sta

ds/

Get your ad on Google today

Be seen by customers at the very moment that they're searching on Google for the things you off and only pay when they click to visit your websit

Google is one of the world's largest technology companies today. It utilizes its position as the world's most popular search engine to sell targeted advertising to companies interested in reaching online consumers. In 2018, Google's advertising revenue was more than $116 billion dollars.

it as an invasion of privacy and are not happy with their browsing history being tracked.[20]

Meanwhile, recent news suggests some advertisers are adjusting their approaches to targeted ads on Facebook. Proctor & Gamble is one such company that has cited limited effectiveness. The company said it would seek new methods of reaching targeted audiences, such as expectant mothers, through websites like Google or YouTube.[21]

Several types of online marketing tactics work thanks to targeted messaging. Among the most popular forms of targeted advertising is via search engine results. Search engine marketing is popular on Google, for example. Google campaigns use the IP address of a computer to market materials specifically to Google users. The search engine tracks the websites a user visits as well as the keywords he or she searches. Google Adwords is a program that also gained prominence in the 2010s. Google and non-Google search partners show ads that match the search results a user finds.

The following essays will discuss some of the major benefits and detriments of targeted advertisements for the average Internet user.

TARGETED ADVERTISEMENTS BENEFIT INTERNET USERS

While targeted advertisements may feel like a nuisance at times, the truth is that they are beneficial for consumers. Naysayers may cite privacy issues when discussing the detriments of targeted advertising, but the truth is that such marketing tactics provide a valuable service that often goes overlooked.

First, consumers benefit from seeing advertisements for products they might be willing to purchase. Instead of viewing generic advertisements that do not pertain to them, web users have customized ads that help them find useful products directly appealing to their specific interests and needs. Thanks to targeted marketing, the relevance of the material shown to you has increased since its advent.

Simply put, targeted advertisements might help you save time. For example, you might type the word "laptop" into your search engine of choice. Before the list of search results, you might notice an advertisement consisting of different laptops for sale through various electronics websites. Clicking on one of these advertisements may direct you to a trustworthy website offering affordable laptops. A specific keyword can tailor the advertisement even more specifically.

Next, advertisements are delivered in the best way to appeal to the web user. The method of ad delivery is in a comfortable, casual manner that fits in with the consumer's specific lifestyle. Even the type of language an

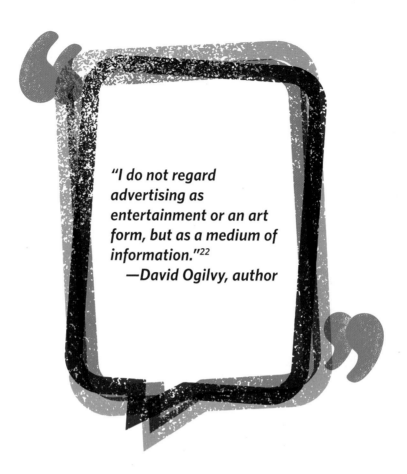

"I do not regard advertising as entertainment or an art form, but as a medium of information."[22]
—David Ogilvy, author

advertisement uses are catered to the target demographic. A professional in his fifties may receive advertisements that are worded differently than the ones viewed by a teenage girl—even if the ad is for the same product. Advertisers know that customization is the key to reaching out to new customers.

Targeted advertisements allow web users to build familiarity with the companies they see ads for. This marketing tactic is beneficial for advertisers, but it also gives consumers peace of mind that the companies they buy products from are reputable. Advertisers engage more often with consumers they target, so this relationship is

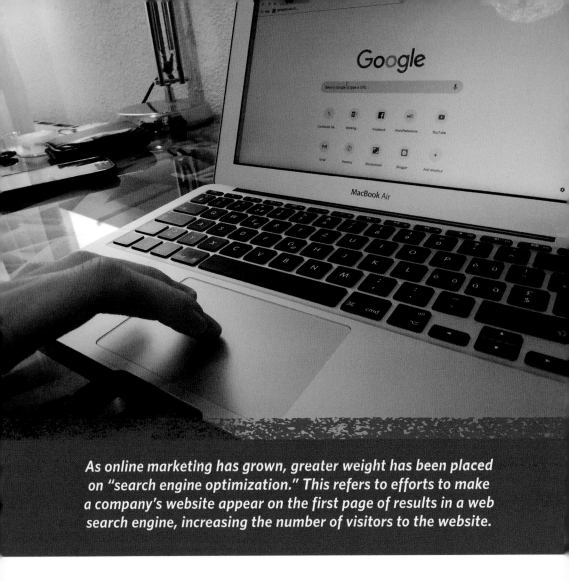

As online marketing has grown, greater weight has been placed on "search engine optimization." This refers to efforts to make a company's website appear on the first page of results in a web search engine, increasing the number of visitors to the website.

mutually beneficial.

Targeted advertisements are also a great opportunity for small businesses that do not have the same reach as the big brands like Amazon or Google. With targeted demographics, small mom and pop businesses have more reach beyond what happens organically on social media.

Also noteworthy is the fact that the Internet would most likely change if the government put a stop to the ability of websites to track its users. For instance, web users would need to log in to see the information they are most interested in. This information would not be as accessible, and the way people use the Internet could slow down considerably. If the alternative to targeted advertisements is a slower, less accessible Internet, which is the better option?

Without cookies and targeted ads, websites may begin to force viewers to sit through longer video advertisements before accessing a website. This experience would be similar to watching trailers before you can see a movie at the theater. This might mean sitting through hours of media each week that does not pertain to the user's interests. Advertisers and consumers would both be wasting their time.

Some people even speculate that without targeted advertisements, web users might see a type of cable television format come to the Internet. This could include different tiers web users would pay to access specific websites. This could wipe out the freedom of the Internet as we know it today. While this is all speculation about what could happen to the Internet, opponents of targeted advertisements must realize that these steps are potential consequences. Companies are going to find a way to advertise regardless of whether they can target specific demographics.

Finally, it is worth considering that even if targeted advertisements were no longer used, companies would still be collecting data. Without restriction, companies may continue to collect data for another use, and the incentive to sell this information may become stronger with fewer opportunities. Would it be possible that unscrupulous organizations would get their hands on personal information about web users? This is certainly a possibility worth considering.

Right now, options exist that make it possible to block targeted ads from showing up on the pages web users visit. Ad blockers do not allow the advertisements to show up on a website, creating a less intrusive environment. This means that people who prefer not to see targeted ads do not have to. Individuals who wish to continue seeing these advertisements may continue to do so.

In addition to targeting individuals on the web based on cookies, some companies have also integrated social media marketing in the form of their own social media profiles. This allows for an additional level of integration and engagement with businesses consumers enjoy. So, social media marketing and targeted advertisements may work hand-in-hand in creating a unique online experience.

The truth is that targeted advertisements are highly useful for both advertisers and customers. The scape of the Internet and the online shopping experience would change significantly without these ads.

Today, approximately 80 percent of all Americans do their shopping online, and more than half say they prefer online shopping to actually visiting a store. Online sales now total approximately $3 billion each year.

TARGETED ADVERTISEMENTS DO NOT BENEFIT INTERNET USERS

Many people are unhappy with the move toward targeted advertisements. In fact, many web users would call it an invasion of privacy because they have not explicitly given permission to somebody else to collect this data. Some websites are tricky about the way they tell users about their privacy policies and tracking methods.

Privacy concerns are among the biggest problems associated with targeted marketing tactics. Sometimes advertisements might even seem too personal. Some people see advertisements and wonder, "How did Google find out that I wanted to buy that?" Targeted advertisements are designed to be specific thanks to **stratified** criteria that narrows down specific products for specific consumers.

Ultimately, web users often feel they are giving too much information to tracking cookies. The information collected about a single user over time can grow intensely. Soon, it may feel that the computer knows every detail about a user's life.

Technology continues to grow each year at an unprecedented rate. Should consumers trust technology they cannot completely understand? Consumers might have a right to feel skeptical about the tracking tactics used to create advertisements. What else could the data be used for? Consumers are not given the full breadth of

"If you could run an ad and reach a million people or run a targeted ad to reach 5,000, you have to have pretty impressive returns on that 5,000 to make it worth it."[23]
—Peter Daboll, CEO of Ace Metrix

information when they visit the websites that track their behaviors, information, and location.

Additionally, targeted advertisements might make it seem that fewer alternative products exist. Eventually, it can feel as if the companies willing to spend the most money are the only ones represented online in targeted advertisements. Companies not spending the money to advertise to targeted markets lack the same representation. Not only do these companies miss out on customers, but consumers also feel they have fewer options.

Also notable is the fact that some researchers have

Because targeted online advertisements are only seen by specific groups of people, they can violate federal laws against discrimination.

discovered that Facebook advertisements have been discriminatory in the past. In fact, several fair housing groups filed a lawsuit against Facebook in 2018, citing discrimination against disabled veterans, women, and single mothers. "We want the court to order Facebook to develop a plan to remove any ability for advertisers to access Facebook's checklists for excluding groups of people in the posting of housing-related ads," an attorney for the group, Diane Houk, told the *New York Times*. "Because of Facebook's impact on the housing market, we'll ask the court to implement a plan of community education and outreach to housing providers to inform them of their obligation not to discriminate."[24] Prior to this lawsuit,

Facebook had previously been accused of violating the Fair Housing Act by targeting housing advertisements so they were shown primarily to white users.

These complaints are just a few examples of the ways that social media sites overstep boundaries and quietly violate laws. If social media websites and advertisers can perform these actions, who is to say that they cannot overreach in other aspects? Considering how often companies like Facebook have been sued, their ability to continue breaking the law even in regards to marketing techniques is notable. Facebook has made tens of billions of dollars selling advertisements on its website, so it makes sense that they may break the law and deal with the consequences rather than avoid letting advertising information be released to the public.

Web users also speak out against the explosion that targeted advertisement became because it is largely invisible to those who don't know about it. These marketing tactics are also difficult to control. The web user cannot do much about the information and data sent to marketing firms. They cannot pick and choose which information they are comfortable sharing. Consumers feel that the situation is "all or nothing." They cannot opt to hide information they would rather not share with advertisers.

One way web users have opted out of targeted advertisements is through the use of ad blockers. While this is often effective in reducing the number of ads web users see, it is an extra step many consumers feel they should not have to take. Since 30 percent of American web users purposefully block advertisements on their computers, it is clear that advertisements have a bad reputation.[25]

The main beneficiary of targeted advertisements are the advertising companies themselves. Studies indicate that companies can expect to receive $2 in revenue for every $1 spent on online advertising, and that revenue from email advertising made up 21 percent of corporate revenue in 2017. Clearly, online advertisements work for many companies. Regardless, many consumers simply aren't comfortable with the knowledge that so many companies are taking their information and spinning it into very personal advertisements.

With so many consumers claiming they are not accepting of targeted advertisements, it is possible that changes may occur in the future. In fact, some organizations are working toward improving privacy for web users around the world.

The truth is that many targeted advertisements pose a complex issue not easily resolved. Companies are going to advertise on the Internet, and web users are looking for products to buy. Unfortunately, there is a third party involved that can make these advertisements more difficult to condone. When greater numbers of people and organizations have access to personal data, it becomes more likely that data will find its way into the wrong hands.

TEXT-DEPENDENT QUESTIONS

1. Name one website that uses targeted advertisements.
2. Who is more likely to have a favorable opinion of targeted advertisements?
3. How much revenue do online advertisements generate each year?
4. What is geotargeting?

RESEARCH PROJECTS

Perform a web search for a common product you might have in your home. Pay close attention to the advertisements that arise on the search results page. Take notes about the ads. What do you notice about them? What kinds of words do the advertisements use in a way to sell products? Are these advertisements effective? Why or why not? Write a short essay describing your experience.

WORDS TO UNDERSTAND

anesthetized—to deprive of awareness or feeling toward something.

procrastination—delaying or postponing something, often something with a negative connotation.

stigma—shame or disgrace associated with a situation, characteristic, or circumstance.

DOES SOCIAL MEDIA USE DETRACT FROM SOCIAL SKILLS AND MENTAL HEALTH?

CHAPTER 4

Social skills encompass a wide variety of the things most people do every day. These are skills people often learn early on, like cooperation and sharing. Children learn participation, patience, and helpfulness from a young age. These skills also include active listening, positive interaction, and courtesy. The popularity of smartphones and social media makes many people wonder if today's social media users are missing out on these important skills.

Imagine speaking to a friend or family member, only to never meet eye contact with him or her. Imagine trying to point to something interesting while on a walk, but the other person is glued to their phone, too busy to look up. For many people, this is a feared future.

When people speak to each other, they have some expectations for how the interaction is going to go. Most people expect some form of eye contact in addition to non-verbal cues like hand movements, raising eyebrows, and shrugging. The basic demonstrations of respect for others are crucial in the world we live in today. Some people believe social media interactions have prompted significant changes in human interaction today.

One 2016 study found that young people and women were more likely to use Facebook intensely, and were more likely to become addicted to Facebook.[26] People who become addicted to social media may exhibit many

CAN SOCIAL SKILLS PREDICT SUCCESS?

Social skills in children and teenagers are also major predictors for success in the future. Children with poor social skills may be at higher risk for bullying, rejection by peers, social isolation, depression, and anxiety. Children who learned skills like conflict resolution in kindergarten were more likely to graduate from college and secure jobs by the time they turned 25. For this reason, many people worry that children who spend too much time on their phones or computers will lack the necessary skills as they grow older.

Social skills do more than facilitate positive relationships with people you care about. Social skills are also called soft skills, and this term is often used to land a job that involves strong social skills. At work, employees need to listen to questions, motivate other

Studies have found that many workers tend to become distracted by social media, leading to lower productivity in their jobs.

these websites. A Chinese study from 2018 found that students who are addicted to social networking sites tend to procrastinate irrationally.[32] Individuals with lower self-regulation and control appeared more affected by irrational procrastination.

Today, it is not uncommon to see people using their phones to check social media while they are performing other tasks or even while watching movies or having dinner with friends. This might lead some to wonder if people can truly live in the moment anymore. Is humanity losing track

Teenagers often value themselves based on comparison with others. At one time, this "peer pressure" was confined to school, but today, thanks to social media apps like Instagram, young people bring this pressure with them wherever they go.

of the present because it is stuck on social media?

In addition to influencing surface social skills, researchers have found that regular social media can actually lower the self-esteem of users. Children who misrepresent themselves on the Internet—for example, by pretending to be older—are less likely to have well-developed social skills and are more likely to have low self-esteem, according to a 2005 study. The researchers found that these children are more likely develop higher levels of aggression and social anxiety.[33] Low self-esteem is a problem that existed long before smartphones and social media, but the new culture of devices makes it harder to identify these problems in young people today.

For young people, their self-esteem can be linked to the images they see on social media networks like Instagram. Teenagers often lack the ability to understand that the Internet offers only a snapshot into somebody else's life. They can develop unrealistic expectations about their lifestyle or their physical appearance based on other posts that they see. Teenagers can feel left out or excluded when they see their classmates posting about parties or fun outings with friends, or feel unappreciated if one of their own posts on social media receives few "likes." Those young people who already have low social-emotional well-being are more likely to experience negative effects associated with social media.

In some cases, social media may even increase suicidal ideation. There is a growing body of evidence that the Internet and social media can influence suicidal thoughts and actions. "There are several specific ways that social media can increase risk for prosuicide behavior. Cyberbullying and cyber harassment, for example, are serious and prevalent problems," write David D. Luxton, Jennifer D. June, and Jonathan M. Fairall in a 2012 study published in the *American Journal of Public Health*. "Cyberbullying typically refers to when a child or adolescent is intentionally and repeatedly targeted by another child or teen in the form of threats or harassments or humiliated or embarrassed by means of cellular phones or Internet technologies such as e-mail, texting, social networking sites, or instant messaging. Cyber harassment and cyber stalking typically refer to these same actions when they involve adults. A review of data collected between 2004 and 2010 via survey studies indicated that lifetime cyberbullying victimization rates ranged from 20.8 percent to 40.6 percent and offending rates ranged from 11.5 percent to 20.1 percent."[34]

Other studies have determined that a history of mental illness had a lot to do with an individual's potential to participate in suicidal ideation. The **stigma** of mental illness does not help either. Many people are afraid to admit that they are living with mental illness because of the way their peers, friends, and family members may react.

Another factor that may increase the rates of attempted and completed suicides is the Werther effect. The Werther effect describes the increasing levels of suicide attempts after the publicly reported death of celebrity or other person. One study suggests that individuals who post online in the wake of a celebrity death exhibit decreased social concerns, more anxiety, and more anger. Social media users may take on a negative, derogatory tone and may describe self-injury or self-harm tendencies.[35]

Keep in mind that suicide is highly influenced by environmental factors. One study of suicide and social media in South Korea demonstrated the role of social affect and social mood on one's likelihood of dying by suicide.

The study also demonstrate that social media variables had taken the place of economic predictors of suicide, like unemployment.[36] Certainly, it is apparently that social media is playing a more significant role in our lives than ever before.

Social media may also subject more people to hate speech. The more people see hate speech in casual conversation, the more they become **anesthetized** to it. Children who grow up seeing racial or homophobic slurs on the Internet or on social networks might develop more casual acceptance this sort of behavior.

In short, it is becoming clear that social media has a negative impact on society and detracts from social skills, especially among young people.

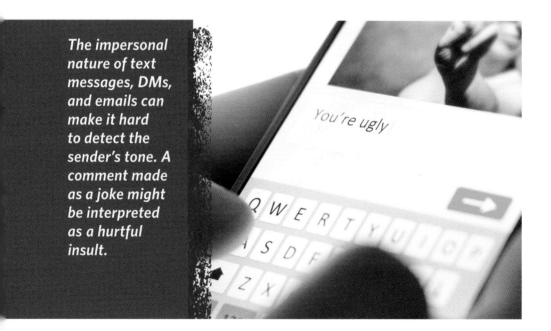

The impersonal nature of text messages, DMs, and emails can make it hard to detect the sender's tone. A comment made as a joke might be interpreted as a hurtful insult.

SOCIAL MEDIA DOES NOT DETRACT
FROM SOCIAL SKILLS

While social media is imperfect, criticisms that these networks hurt the development of social skills in young people are not fair. In fact, some experts believe that social media can actually enhance social skills for the young people who use it wisely.

In fact, in a 2018 study by Common Sense Media, more teens reported that they benefited from social media than those who reported negative consequences. The survey found that 25 percent of teens felt less money when they used social media, compared to 3 percent who felt more lonely. Twenty percent felt more confident using social media, compared to 5 percent who felt less confident.[37] Vulnerable teenagers may benefit from social media even more because they can relate to friends and family members through the networks even if they do not have physical access to others at a particular time.

Simply because people are on their phones does not mean they are not engaging others socially. Many people use social media to socialize with friends, just in a different manner than their parents are used to. A teenager who appears to be lost in the phone might actually be having a bonding experience with a close friend from school. The activities teens and young adults do on their phones are not always mindless. Teenagers can use their smartphones to check their grades, communicate with educators, and

According to a 2018 survey by the Pew Research Center, more than 80 percent of teens reported that social media helped them feel more connected to their friends. Over 67 percent said social networks helped them to interact with a more diverse group of people and made them feel as though they had a support system during difficult times.

even apply for schools. Phones are crucial tools today, not just avenues to fun and games.

The exposure of people to new ideas brought on by the Internet is largely beneficial for improving social skills and strengthening relationships. For one, social media can overcome geographical barriers to communication.

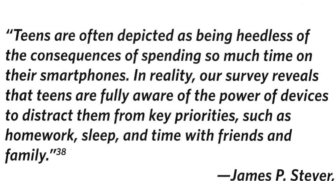

"Teens are often depicted as being heedless of the consequences of spending so much time on their smartphones. In reality, our survey reveals that teens are fully aware of the power of devices to distract them from key priorities, such as homework, sleep, and time with friends and family."[38]

—James P. Steyer,
founder and CEO of Common Sense Media

Strengthening relationships may include sending pictures back and forth, sharing details about their day, and discussing current events. Smartphones offer a variety of media through which people can share their lives with their loved ones, including video chatting and online games. Bonding experiences have changed over time, but they still exist.

Teenagers are also often the first people to admit that social media can be a distraction. The Common Sense Media study showed that 70 percent of teenagers use social media two or more times per day. Most teens admitted to understanding that social media networks manipulate users so that they will spend more time on their devices.[39] Adults may not give teenagers enough credit when it comes to acknowledging the use of technological devices and social media. Teenagers who have grown up surrounded by new technology can often see right through the tricks these networks try to pull. Often, adults who are new to technology are more likely to be taken in by these manipulative strategies.

Studies also demonstrate that cyberbullying is less common than many people believe. About 13 percent of teenagers surveyed by Common Sense Media in 2018 reported experiencing cyberbullying, and about 9 percent reported that the cyberbullying was serious.[40] This is tragic and troubling, but it also means that roughly 90 percent of teenagers will not experience serious cyberbullying during their lives. Most teenagers fear real-life bullying more than anything they experience on the web. When cyberbullying does become an issue, teenagers can alert authorities or adults to the problem so that they can take action. Parents who monitor their children's social media are more likely to spot the signs of potential bullying.

Additionally, social media provides a way for young people to find support for their problems. Support networks can help people with chronic illness, mental health issues, and even small life problems. People can find others who have been through similar challenges and speak to them. For teenagers going through the changes associated with adolescence, having peers to reach out to can be significant. This is especially important considering that teens are more likely to reach out on the web rather than in person, which can feel awkward and embarrassing. Social media facilitates support groups and other ways to reach out.

Social skills now also include the ability to network on the web. How many jobs these days ask their applicants if they are well-versed in typing and networking online? It may very well be the case that today's students who have grown up with increasing technology are better equipped for the workforce.

Finally, about 27 percent of teenagers report that they use social media as a means of creative expression.[41] They benefit emotionally and mentally from being able to share their art on the web. It is through the web that teens grow their expressive skills. Teenagers who have an easier time discussing their feelings on the web may be able to discuss their issues more clearly in person too. Building the freedom to talk about their feelings on the web can help many teenagers find their voice.

Many people fear that teenagers on their phones are going to create problems for socializing in the future. The truth is that teenagers may actually be developing new social skills that older generations never had. The changing scope of socialization may not be a bad thing. It may just be different.

TEXT-DEPENDENT QUESTIONS

1. What is one option for helping people who lack social skills?
2. How can social media assist individuals with chronic pain?
3. What does it mean to be afraid of social stigma?
4. What is the Werther effect? How does it relate to social media?

 RESEARCH PROJECTS

Do you think social media is good or bad for social skills and mental health? Find three pieces of evidence supporting your opinion. Now, find three facts that support the opposite viewpoint. Do these opposing viewpoints change your opinion? Write a short essay in which you explain why or why not.

doxing—to search for and publish identifying information about a person on the Internet, typically in a malicious manner.

unscrupulous—the quality of lacking moral principles and ethics. Dishonest or unfair.

privacy policy—a statement of document disclosing what information a company gathers, how it discloses information, and what it does to manage private data.

DOES SOCIAL MEDIA REVEAL TOO MUCH?

CHAPTER 5

After Facebook faced public scrutiny for allowing Cambridge Analytica to have access to user data in 2018, more social media users began to worry whether they were revealing too much about themselves on the Internet. In fact, many people began to wonder if they should leave social media altogether. Most people use social media to stay in touch with people they care about—not to share their data.

One study in 2014 discovered that more than 90 percent of Americans believed that people had lost control over how their personal information is collected and used by a variety of entities, including social media websites. About 80 percent of social media users claimed they felt concerned that advertisers and businesses were accessing their social media data, and about 64 percent wished the government would do more to regulate this action.[42] Currently, the government takes some actions to preserve consumer data, but the fact that targeted advertisements exists is a concern for many web users.

The sheer truth of the matter is that many people have no idea what information they share that is then shared through other channels. There is simply no way to track where this information goes, especially when people use social media frequently. Most people have shared information to other websites that they didn't necessarily know was going to be spread elsewhere.

The information displayed on social media websites like Facebook is a problem too. According to a 2018 article by the Pew Research Center, "91 percent of Americans 'agree'

WHAT'S IN A NAME?

Unfortunately, many people are not aware of the many things they do on the web or the features they interact with that could put them at risk. If you have encountered any of these privacy risks on the web, you could be putting yourself at higher risk for privacy invasion.

Malware is a type of software that puts your computer and information at risk. Malware includes viruses and Trojan horses. It can also include spyware, which delves into your computer to seek out information like your usernames and passwords.

Phishing is another common practice. Many people receive phishing emails that appear to come from a legitimate company or organization, like a bank or government organization. When the web user clicks or 'strongly agree' that people have lost control over how personal information is collected and used by all kinds of entities. Some 80 percent of social media users said they were concerned about advertisers and businesses accessing the data they share on social media platforms, and 64 percent said the government should do more to regulate advertisers."[43]

In spite of distrust toward social media platforms, many people still have profiles on Facebook and other networks. This brings up an intriguing question about the expectations people have for social media. If companies like Facebook should not be trusted, why do people

on a link in the email, it will take them to a website that looks just like the organization's website. When the user inputs their email address and password, the phisher will use that information to log in through the actual website.

Sometimes simply using a weak password or the same password on every website is the highest security risk a person takes regularly. Weak passwords include those without numbers, those without uppercase letters, and those that include words like your first name, pet's name, or the word "password."

When you understand the potential ways you could put yourself at risk, you can make better decisions for your Internet security and privacy.

continue to input their information? Why do people choose to share their personal information, even when they do not trust the companies that run the social networks?

While the Pew study found nearly 60 percent of users said they would not have a difficult time giving up social media, the number of users who feel this would be difficult has increased. In spite of the untrustworthy reputation, people have grown reliant on social media to keep up with the day-to-day lives of family members and friends.

Unfortunately, social media websites can also make it difficult for users to change their privacy controls. A recent survey found that nearly half of users claimed they had a hard time managing their privacy settings.[44] In fact, the survey indicated that millions of people may not even realize that Facebook has privacy settings they can manage.

Scan here to see a former Facebook executive warn about social media use.

Managing privacy settings is an important aspect of safely using social media networks like Facebook.

It's not only corporations and marketing agencies that people worry about when they think about social media. Social media users are also considered about the role these websites could play in making them victims of crimes, like kidnapping, harassment, or robbery. They also worry about the role social media websites could play in landing (or losing) a job or a place at a university. Even when a person is diligent about their privacy settings, once information is posted to another site that person will never have total control over it anymore.

Privacy on the web is by no means a simple issue. The following essays will discuss whether social media enables users to reveal too much about themselves, or if social media companies provide appropriate privacy controls.

SOCIAL MEDIA REVEALS TOO MUCH INFORMATION

It makes sense that privacy is a growing concern in the world today. At times, it may feel that the universe is becoming one large advertisement. Increasingly, it becomes easy to feel that the Internet exists merely to study each person and then create advertisements targeted for each individual.

Of course, privacy and marketing are not the only issues at stake in the world today. In fact, privacy is becoming larger in a social context as well. Today, many social media users worry that they are revealing way too much information about themselves and their families on the Internet. And then, there are people who don't realize what they are sharing online.

Today, some people have trouble differentiating between information appropriate for an online environment and information they should keep to themselves. This is becoming a problem that extends beyond the role advertisers may play in gathering data because people may not realize they are actually publishing personal data they do not want the rest of the world to see.

One problem arising is with the advent of "mommy bloggers." Some parents share information about their children that they do not realize could cross privacy boundaries. When the child grows older, he or she may realize that a parent posted their personal healthcare information or even data like a birthday or last name, which can be used to obtain personal documents later on.

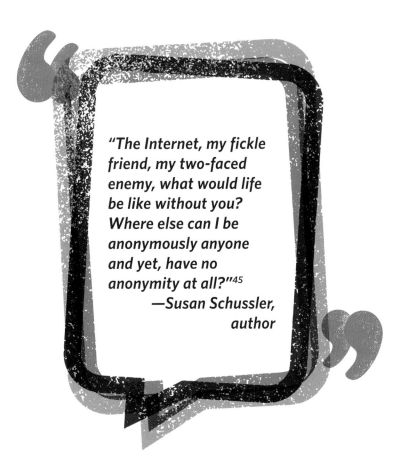

"The Internet, my fickle friend, my two-faced enemy, what would life be like without you? Where else can I be anonymously anyone and yet, have no anonymity at all?"[45]
—Susan Schussler, author

Then, there is the fact that children can share information with hundreds or thousands of people without realizing what they have posted is inappropriate. Children lack many of the decision-making skills that develop through adolescence, so they may not realize that posting an address online is a major security issue.

Even teenagers often fail to realize that they should be more concerned with privacy issues on the web. Less than 10 percent of teen Facebook users studied claimed they felt any concern about privacy on the web.[46] This level of confidence could be dangerous. For example, more than three-fourths of teenagers have posted the names of their schools online.[47] These teens may not realize that posting such information could mean that somebody with bad intentions could actually see this information.

Any photo posted online could provide **unscrupulous** individuals with the opportunity for **doxing**. About 91 percent of teenagers surveyed had posted photos of themselves online.[48] Often, small details in a picture can provide clues to somebody on the Internet. Address numbers on a house, a book with the name of a high school, or the background at a local park can provide insight to somebody who wants to find out where you are.

Some websites encourage their users to post photos of strangers without their consent. Some people in the past have become unintentionally famous, sometimes for something they did not actually mean to do. Unfortunately, this can lead to embarrassment, real-life bullying, and cyberbullying. Many people regret becoming famous on the Internet for these reasons.

One of the biggest problems with social media is that it spreads information so quickly. Much of the information spread on these platforms is unreliable, unverifiable, or completely false. In fact, 64 percent of users on Twitter looking for news expressed they found information on the website that later turned out to be totally false.[49] Not only that, but lies on Twitter tends to spread about six times faster than truthful information.[50] This fact means it is very easy to disseminate false information on the Internet, but correcting these falsehoods can be infinitely more difficult.

Additionally, social media can harm an individual's job stability or even a person's ability to procure a job entirely. Social media profiles that reveal profanity, poor grammar, sexual content, or references to illegal drugs may lead to professional rejection. Employers have a legal right to fire individuals who may put the company's reputation at risk online.

Another problem is that social media can reveal information to criminals and other individuals who might use the information your present in an untoward manner. For example, sex offenders could use social media websites to speak with potential victims. Others may examine social media websites to look for people claiming they are on vacation so that they can then rob an empty house. People often do not think twice about posting pictures from vacation, but it can have ramifications.

In the past, location services on websites like Facebook have also create dangers for activists, journalists, and even the military. For example, a soldier or journalist with their location services settings turned on could accidentally reveal an information to an enemy or somebody who seeks to do harm. In settings like these, paying attention to privacy could be a life-or-death situation.

And then, there are the privacy policies of advertisers who use Facebook to look for information. When a Facebook users clicks a button to give a website access to view their social media profile, the information advertisers glean is more than meets the eye. Advertisers can learn about your occupation, Google searches, age range, gender, and location. Knowing that marketing companies have this amount of information about you can be frightening.

Finally, social media users should keep in mind that nothing is truly deleted form the Internet. In fact, the Library of Congress has been archiving many public Tweets since 2006. The public posts you make could be saved forever, and you have no power over how these posts are used by media in the future.

Unfortunately, social media opens too many doors that cannot easily be closed. While many people may not care that advertisers have access to their personal data, they should be concerned that other social media users have access to compromising information.

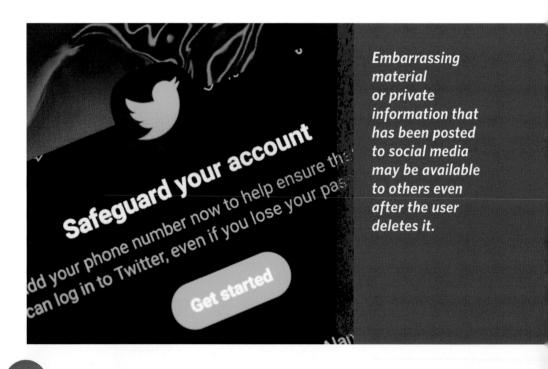

Embarrassing material or private information that has been posted to social media may be available to others even after the user deletes it.

SOCIAL MEDIA DOES NOT REVEAL
TOO MUCH INFORMATION

The truth about social media is that people are not forced to share anything they are not comfortable with. People who use social media understand the risks they face when they use the websites, so it is not the fault of social media when something goes wrong.

One argument could be that people need to understand the limitations of privacy in an online world. People with nothing to hide should not be concerned that their information may be used by advertisers or the government. The majority of people are not targeted for information by the government, especially if they have not done anything illegal.

Teenagers tend to understand the necessity for privacy. In fact, 60 percent of teenage Facebook users have private profiles. Teenagers tend to report that they are "confident they can manage their privacy settings."[51] Additionally, teenagers who use social media tend to develop a strong sense of reputation management. They understand how to delete people from their networks when they are not comfortable. Today's generations of teenagers understand the way social media works more than many adults. While dangers can present on the web, parents can teach their children how to spot the signs that something is wrong.

Not only do people check social media for personal updates from friends, but they also check it for breaking news. For many people, social media websites like

"We shouldn't ask our customers to make a tradeoff between privacy and security. We need to offer them the best of both. Ultimately, protecting someone else's data protects all of us."[52]

—Tim Cook, CEO of Apple

Facebook are the top news source. In fact, social media has played a significant role in breaking major news events, including the Aurora, Colorado, theater shooting in 2012. Today, people rely on social media websites to learn information about the world around them. While the news might break stories too early to be completely accurate, the good news is that people who use social media will be alerted when something is wrong.

Thanks to some of the information people reveal on the web, law enforcement has been able to catch and prosecute criminals efficiently. Today, many law enforcement professionals believe that social media is beneficial for solving crimes quickly.[53] Believe it or not, all too many criminals post about their crimes on the web. People who obey the law do not need to worry about the police presence on social media, nor do they need to worry about their posts being used in a criminal court setting.

It is true that children and teenagers are among the most vulnerable people on the Internet. Thankfully, age restrictions have been implemented by the government to ensure that young children are not legally allowed to provide information to websites looking for it. Additionally, states like California have passed laws to protect the privacy of adolescents by allowing minors to erase their own comments from certain types of websites.

Parents also have a responsibility and right to monitor the Internet usage of their children. Parents often need to step in and teach their children about safety on the web, but they often don't. Rather than blame social media websites for the information children post, laws might instead seek to hold parents responsible for any safety risks their children face by posting online. Social media websites do their part by implementing rules for their websites.

Additionally, many states have passed laws against cyberstalking. People who use social media to stalk users face repercussions just like people who stalk others through other means. One of the central problems is the lack of reporting issues like cyberstalking to the authorities.

In addition to realizing the availability of laws regarding cyberstalking, it is also important to realize that stalking happens in real life as well. Social media is just one of many tools a person might use to stalk or harass another person.

In the end, it is up to social media users to come to their own conclusions about the privacy policies of the websites they visit. Websites are required to update their visitors when the **privacy policy** changes. If people opt out of reading pertinent information about the social media websites they visit, this is not the fault of the social media websites. Consumers have the responsibility to read the information before agreeing to use the website.

Ultimately, people still have the right to post only the information they feel comfortable with. While some people might choose to post more information than others on social media, this is not the fault of social media websites.

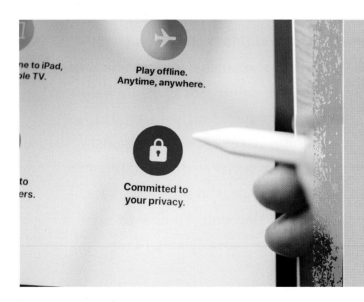

In recent years, social networks and technology companies have added new tools to protect the privacy of online users.

TEXT-DEPENDENT QUESTIONS

1. What percentage of people surveyed claimed they did not completely trust the information posted online?
2. What is a privacy policy?
3. How quickly does false information spread on Twitter compared to true information?
4. What percentage of teenagers have posted photos of themselves on the Internet?

RESEARCH PROJECTS

Research a case in the news in which an individual or group of individuals had their privacy breached. This could be a case involving marketing, cyberstalking, cyberbullying, robbery, or any other security or privacy issue mentioned in this chapter. Then, write a short paper describing the situation and what could have prevented privacy or security from breach.

affidavit—a sworn statement, in writing, that sets out a person's testimony.

affirmative action programs—programs that are intended to improve the educational or employment opportunities of members of minority groups and women.

BCE and CE—alternatives to the traditional Western designation of calendar eras, which used the birth of Jesus as a dividing line. BCE stands for "Before the Common Era," and is equivalent to BC ("Before Christ"). Dates labeled CE, or "Common Era," are equivalent to Anno Domini (AD, or "the Year of Our Lord").

colony—a country or region ruled by another country.

democracy—a country in which the people can vote to choose those who govern them.

discrimination—prejudiced outlook, action, or treatment, often in a negative way.

detention center—a place where people claiming asylum and refugee status are held while their case is investigated.

ethnic cleansing—an attempt to rid a country or region of a particular ethnic group. The term was first used to describe the attempt by Serb nationalists to rid Bosnia of Muslims.

felony—a serious crime; in the United States, a felony is any crime for which the punishment is more than one year in prison or the death penalty.

fundamentalist—beliefs based on a strict biblical or scriptural interpretation of religious law.

median—In statistics, the number that falls in the center of a group, meaning half the numbers are higher than the number and half are lower.

minority—a part of a population different from the majority in some characteristics and often subjected to differential treatment.

paranoia—a mental disorder characterized by the strong belief that the person is being unfairly persecuted.

parole—releasing someone sentenced to prison before the full sentence is served, granted for good behavior.

plaintiff—a person making a complaint in a legal case in civil court.

pro bono—a Latin phrase meaning "for the public good," referring to legal work undertaken without payment or at a reduced fee as a public service.

racial profiling—projecting the characteristics of a few people onto the entire population of a group; for example, when police officers stop people on suspicion of criminal activity solely because of their race.

racism—discrimination against a particular group of people based solely on their racial background.

segregation—the separation or isolation of a race, class, or group from others in society. This can include restricting areas in which members of the race, class, or group can live; placing barriers to social interaction; separate educational facilities; or other discriminatory means.

ORGANIZATIONS TO CONTACT

A Platform for Good
Website: http://aplatformforgood.org/

Common Sense Media
2200 Pennsylvania Avenue, NW,
4th Floor East
Washington, D.C. 20037
Phone: (202) 350-9992
Website: www.commonsensemedia.org

Crimes Against Children Research Center
University of New Hampshire
15 Academic Way #125
McConnell Hall Durham, NH 03824
Phone: (603) 862-3541
Website: www.unh.edu/ccrc/index.html

Cyberbullying Research Center
Website: https://cyberbullying.org

Electronic Privacy Information Center
1718 Connecticut Avenue, NW, Suite 200
Washington, DC 20009
Phone: (202) 483-1140
Website: https://www.epic.org

Federal Communications Commission
445 12th Street SW
Washington, DC, 20554
Phone: (888) 255-5322
Website: https://www.fcc.gov

Family Online Safety Institute
1440 G Street NW
Washington, DC 20005
Phone: (202) 775-0158
Website: https://www.fosi.org

iKeepSafe
c/o Leavitt Partners
601 New Jersey Avenue NW, Suite 350
Washington, DC 20001
Phone: (540) 385-9862
Website: https://ikeepsafe.org

Privacy International
62 Britton Street
London, EC1M 5UY, United Kingdom
Website: www.privacyinternational.org

US Federal Privacy Council
Phone: (202) 829-3660
Website: www.fpc.gov

FURTHER READING

Alderman, Ellen, and Caroline Kennedy. *The Right to Privacy*. New York: Vintage Books, 2010.

Alter, Adam. *Irresistible: The Rise of Addictive Technology and the Business of Keeping Us Hooked*. New York: Penguin, 2018.

Brin, David. *The Transparent Society: Will Technology Force Us to Choose between Privacy and Freedom?* New York: Perseus Books, 1998.

Calvert, Clay. *Voyeur Nation: Media, Privacy, and Peering in Modern Culture*. New York: Westview Press, 2000.

Goodman, Marc. *Future Crimes: Everything Is Connected, Everyone Is Vulnerable, and What We Can Do About It*. New York: Anchor Books, 2015.

Greenwald, Glenn. *No Place to Hide: Edward Snowden, the NSA, and the US Surveillance State*. New York: Metropolitan Books, 2014.

Kirkpatrick, David. *The Facebook Effect*. London: Virgin, 2011.

Li, Qing, Donna Cross, and Peter K. Smith. *Cyberbullying in the Global Playground: Research from International Perspectives*. Hoboken: Wiley-Blackwell, 2012.

Littman, Sarah Darer. *Backlash*. New York: Scholastic, 2015.

McKee, Jonathan. *The Teen's Guide to Social Media and Mobile Devices*. USA: Shiloh Run Press, 2017.

Mitnick, Kevin. *The Art of Invisibility: The World's Most Famous Hacker Teaches You How to Be Safe in the Age of Big Brother and Big Data*. New York: Little, Brown and Company, 2017.

Pang, Alex Soojung-Kim. *The Distraction Addiction: Getting the Information You Need and the Communication You Want, Without Enraging Your Family, Annoying Your Colleagues, and Destroying Your Soul*. New York: Little, Brown and Company, 2013.

Poland, Bailey. *Haters: Harassment, Abuse, and Violence Online*. Lincoln: Potomac Books, 2016.

Shariff, Shaheen. *Cyber-Bullying: Issues and Solutions for the School, the Classroom and the Home*. London: Routledge, 2008.

Solove, Daniel, J. *Nothing to Hide: The False Tradeoff between Privacy and Security*. New Haven: Yale University Press, 2011.

INTERNET RESOURCES

https://cyberbullying.org/cyberbullying-victimization-rates-2016
This chart shows the rates of cyberbullying victimization by race, age, and sex. This resource breaks down victimization into different groups so visitors can understand who is at higher risk for cyberbullying.

https://staysafeonline.org/stay-safe-online/managing-your-privacy/
Stay Safe Online offers resources for learning about managing your privacy on the Internet. Links are available for teenagers who want to manage their social media usage.

https://www.stopbullying.gov/respond/on-the-spot/index.html
This resources addresses bullying in real-life, but it also shines a spotlight on how people can respond to bullying in any form.

https://www.cbsnews.com/pictures/then-and-now-a-history-of-social-networking-sites/
This resource offers a rich history of social media websites, allowing you to understand the timeline of history leading to today's social networking hotspots.

https://www.stopbullying.gov/laws/index.html
This website lists each state and links to specific laws regarding cyberbullying for each location. With a glance, users can view which states have laws, which have policies, and which states implement both.

https://www.safesearchkids.com/a-teens-guide-to-social-media-safety/
On this website, teens can find different guides that help them navigate social media. The website presents safety tips for avoiding common social media problems.

https://www.pacer.org/bullying/resources/info-facts.asp
This resource answers frequently asked questions about bullying and cyberbullying. Here, readers can learn the difference between bullying and harassment, the role of peer pressure in cyberbullying, and how parents can react to cyberbullying.

CHAPTER NOTES

1 Edward Snowden, quoted in Laura Poitras and Glenn Greenwald, "Edward Snowden: 'The US Government Will Say I Aided our Enemies'," *The Guardian* (July 8, 2013). https://www.theguardian.com/world/video/2013/jul/ 08/edward-snowden-video-interview

2 Charles Mahtesian, "Privacy in Retreat, A Timeline," National Public Radio (June 11, 2013). https://www.npr.org/ 2013/06/11/190721205/privacy-in-retreat-a-timeline

3 Barack Obama, "Statement by the President," The White House, Office of the Press Secretary (June 7, 2013). https:// obamawhitehouse.archives.gov/the-press-office/2013/06/07/statement-president

4 Jerry Kang, "Information Privacy in Cyberspace Transactions," *Stanford Law Review* 5, no. 4 (April 1998). p. 1193. www.jstor.org/stable/1229286.

5 Monica Anderson and Jingjing Jiang, "Teens, Social Media and Technology 2018," Pew Research Center (May 31, 2018). http://www.pewinternet.org/2018/05/31/ teens-social-media-technology-2018/

6 Robert S. Tokunaga, "Following You Home from School: A Critical Review and Synthesis of Research on Cyberbullying Victimization," *Computers in Human Behavior* 26, no. 3 (March 2010), p. 277. https:// www.sciencedirect.com/science/article/pii/S074756320900185X

7 Amanda Lenhart, "Cyberbullying," Pew Research Center (June 27, 2007). http:// www.pewinternet.org/2007/06/27/ cyberbullying/

8 Jonathan Nakomoto and David Schwartz, "Is Peer Victimization Associated with Academic Achievement? A Meta-analytic Review," *Social Development* 19, no. 2 (2010), p. 221. https://onlinelibrary.wiley.com/doi/abs/10.1111/j. 1467-9507.2009.00539.x

9 Amanda Lenhart, "Cyberbullying."

10 American Academy of Pediatrics policy statement, "Children, Adolescents, and the Media," (2013). pediatrics.aappublications.org/content/pediatrics/132/5/958.full.pdf

11 Society for Personality and Social Psychology, "Declining Loneliness Among American Teenagers," (accessed January 9, 2019). http://www.spsp.org/news-center/press-releases/declining-loneliness-among-american-teenagers

12 Sheri Gordon, "Surprising Ways Your Teen Benefits From Social Media," Very Well Family (March 29, 2019). https://www.verywellfamily.com/benefits-of-social-media-4067431

13 Martin Paulus, quoted in Sara Kiley Watson, "A Look At Social Media Finds Some Possible Benefits For Kids," National Public Radio (June 19, 2018). https://www.npr.org/sections/health-shots/2018/06/19/621136346/a-look-at- social-media-finds-some-possible-benefits-for-kids

CHAPTER NOTES

[14] Dr. Catherine Steiner-Adair, quoted in Rachel Emke, "How Using Social Media Affects Teenagers," Child Mind (accessed January 5, 2019). https://childmind.org/article/how-using-social-media-affects-teenagers/

[15] Committee on Adolescent Health Care, "Adolescence," The American College of Obstetricians and Gynecologists (2016). https:// www.acog.org/Clinical-Guidance-and-Publications/Committee-Opinions/Committee-on-Adolescent-Health-Care/Concerns-Regarding-Social-Media-and-Health-Issues-in-Adolescents-and-Young-Adults

[16] C. Sabina, J. Wolak, and D. Finkelhor, "The Nature and Dynamics of Internet Pornography Exposure for Youth," *Cyberpsychology Behavior* 11, no. 6 (June 2008). https://www.ncbi.nlm.nih.gov/pubmed/18771400

[17] Kai Yuan, et al., "Microstructure Abnormalities in Adolescents with Internet Addiction Disorder," *PLOS One* (2011). https://journals.plos.org/plosone/article?id=10.1371/journal.pone.0020708

[18] Caitlyn Fuller, Eric Lehmen, Steven Hicks, and Marsha B. Novick, " Bedtime Use of Technology and Associated Sleep Problems in Children," *Global Pediatric Health* (2017). https://journals.sagepub.com/doi/full/ 10.1177/2333794X17736972

[19] Jean M. Twenge, Thomas E. Joiner, Megan L. Rogers, and Gabrielle N. Martin, "Increases in Depressive Symptoms, Suicide-Related Outcomes, and Suicide Rates Among U.S. Adolescents After 2010 and Links to Increased New Media Screen Time," *Clinical Psychological Science* (2017). https://journals.sagepub.com/doi/full/ 10.1177/2167702617723376

[20] Russell Heimlich, "Internet Users Don't Like Targeted Ads," Pew Research Center (March 13, 2012). http:// www.pewresearch.org/fact-tank/2012/03/13/internet-users-dont-like-targeted-ads/

[21] Sharon Terlep and Deepa Seetheraman, "P&G to Scale Back Targeted Facebook Ads," *The Wall Street Journal* (August 17, 2016). https://www.wsj.com/articles/p-g-to-scale-back-targeted-facebook-ads-1470760949

[22] David Ogilvy, *Ogilvy on Advertising* (New York: Vintage Books, 1983), p. 16.

[23] Peter Daboll, quoted in Terlep and Seetheraman, "P&G to Scale Back Targeted Facebook Ads."

[24] Diana Houk, quoted in Charles V. Bagli, "Facebook Vowed to End Discriminatory Housing Ads. Suit Says It Didn't," *The New York Times* (March 27, 2018). https://www.nytimes.com/2018/03/27/nyregion/facebook-housing- ads-discrimination-lawsuit.html

[25] Statista, "Ad Blocking User Penetration Rate in the United States from 2014 to 2018," (accessed January 8, 2019). https://www.statista.com/statistics/804008/ad-blocking-reach-usage-us/

[26] Aneta Przepiorka, Agata Bachnio, and Juan F. Daz-Morales, "Problematic

Facebook Use and Procrastination," *Computers in Human Behavior* 65 (December 2016). https://dl.acm.org/citation.cfm?id=3075757

[27] Alexis Blue, "Poor Social Skills May Be Harmful to Mental and Physical Health," University of Arizona News (November 6, 2017). https://uanews.arizona.edu/story/poor-social-skills-may-be-harmful-mental-and-physical-health

[28] Chris Segrin, quoted in Blue, "Poor Social Skills May Be Harmful to Mental and Physical Health."

[29] Brianna Steinhilber, "Four Exercises to Combat 'Text Neck'," NBC News (January 24, 2018). https://www.nbcnews.com/better/ health/4-neck-exercises-will-counteract-effects-texting-ncna840291

[30] Roman Prem, Tabea E. Scheel, Oliver Weigelt, Katja Hoffman, and Christian Korunka, "Procrastination in Daily Working Life: A Diary Study on Within-Person Processes That Link Work Characteristics to Workplace Procrastination," *Frontiers in Psychology* 9 (2018). https://www.ncbi.nlm.nih.gov/pmc/articles/PMC6042014/

[31] Przepiorka, Bachnio, and Daz-Morales, "Problematic Facebook Use and Procrastination."

[32] Shuai-lei Lian, et al., "Social Networking Site Addiction and Undergraduate Students' Irrational Procrastination: The mediating role of social networking site fatigue and the moderating role of effortful control," *PLOS One* (2018). https://journals.plos.org/plosone/article? id=10.1371/journal.pone.0208162

[33] Jeffrey P. Harman, Catherine E. Hansen, Margaret E. Cochran, and Cynthia R. Lindsey, "Liar, Liar: Internet Faking but Not Frequency of Use Affects Social Skills, Self-Esteem, Social Anxiety, and Aggression," *CyberPsychology and Behavior* 8, no. 1 (January 2005). https://www.liebertpub.com/doi/abs/10.1089/cpb.2005.8.1

[34] David D. Luxton, Jennifer D. June, and Jonathan M. Fairall, "Social Media and Suicide: A Public Health Perspective," *American Journal of Public Health* 102, no. S2 (May 1, 2012). https://ajph.aphapublications.org/doi/ abs/10.2105/AJPH.2011.300608

[35] Mrinal Kumar, Mark Dredze, Glen Coppersmith, and Munmun de Choudhury, "Detecting Changes in Suicide Content Manifested in Social Media Following Celebrity Suicides," Proceedings of the 26th ACM Conference on Hypertext & Social Media (2015). https://dl.acm.org/citation.cfm?id=2791026

[36] Hong-Hee Won, Woojae Myung, Gil-Young Song, Won-Hee Lee, Jong-Won Kim, Bernard J. Carroll, and Doh Kwan Kim, "Predicting National Suicide Numbers with Social Media Data," *PLOS One* (2013). https:// journals.plos.org/plosone/article?id=10.1371/journal.pone.0061809

[37] Common Sense Media, "Social Media, Social Life: Teens Reveal Their Experiences 2018." (accessed January 3, 2019). https://www.commonsensemedia.org/research/social-media-social-life-2018

CHAPTER NOTES

[38] James P. Steyer, quoted in Common Sense Media, "Social Media, Social Life: Teens Reveal Their Experiences 2018."

[39] Common Sense Media, "Social Media, Social Life."

[40] Common Sense Media, "Social Media, Social Life."

[41] Common Sense Media, "Social Media, Social Life."

[42] Lee Rainie, "Americans' Complicated Feelings About Social Media in an Era of Privacy Concerns," FactTank (March 27, 2018). http://www.pewresearch.org/fact-tank/2018/03/27/americans-complicated-feelings-about-social-media-in-an-era-of- privacy-concerns/

[43] Rainie, "Americans' Complicated Feelings About Social Media in an Era of Privacy Concerns."

[44] Rainie, "Americans' Complicated Feelings About Social Media in an Era of Privacy Concerns."

[45] Susan Schussler, *Between the Raindrops* (Rocky Shore Media, 2013), p. 72.

[46] Madden, Mary, Amanda Lenhart, Sandra Cortesi, Urs Gasser, Maeve Duggan, Aaron Smith, and Meredith Beaton, "Teens, Social Media, and Privacy," Pew Research Center (May 21, 2013) assets.pewresearch.org/wp-content/uploads/sites/14/2013/05/PIP_TeensSocialMediaandPrivacy_PDF.pdf

[47] Madden, Mary, et al., "Teens, Social Media, and Privacy."

[48] Madden, Mary, et al., "Teens, Social Media, and Privacy."

[49] Tom Rosenstiel, Jeff Sonderman, Kevin Loker, Maria Ivancin, and Nina Kjarval, "Twitter and the News: How People Use the Social Network to Learn About the World," American Press Institute (2015). https:// www.americanpressinstitute.org/publications/reports/survey-research/how-people-use-twitter-news/

[50] Soroush Vosoughi, Deb Roy, and Sinan Aral, "The Spread of True and False News Online," *Science Magazine* 259 (2018). http://science.sciencemag.org/content/359/6380/1146

[51] Madden, Mary, et al., "Teens, Social Media, and Privacy."

[52] Tim Cook, quoted in Kaspersky Lab Daily blog, "10 Best Quotes from Tim Cook's Recent Speech on Privacy and Security," (June 3, 2015). https://usa.kaspersky.com/blog/tim-cook-speaks-about-privacy-security/5391/

[53] Sarah M. Wojcik, "More Departments Utilizing Facebook to Catch Criminals," *Police One* (2016). https:// www.policeone.com/social-media-for-cops/articles/181012006-More-departments-utilizing-Facebook-to-catch-criminals/

INDEX

academic performance, 29, 40, 76
Ace Metrix, 59
active marketing, 49
    See also targeted advertising
ad blockers, 61–62, 104
addiction, 39, 66–67, 104
adolescents, 26–41, 65–66, 79–80
    See also social media; social skills
advertising, 16–17, 20, 45–51
    See also targeted advertising
aggression, 72
alcohol abuse, 39
Amazon, 54
American Academy of Pediatrics (AAP), 30, 103
American Journal of Public Health, 73
Annenberg School of Communications, 48–49
anxiety, 29, 66, 68, 72, 74
Apple, Inc., 94
ARPANET, 8–10
authority, 67

bank account, 19
bed-wetting, 29
Berners-Lee, Timothy, 11
Bing, 48
blogging, 88
bots, 17–18
browsing habits, 20–21, 37–38, 45–51
    See also personal information
bullying. *See* cyberbullying
Bush, George W., 23

Cambridge Analytics, 23–24, 83
catfishing, 42
    See also misrepresentation
child pornography, 39
chronic pain, 68
circadian rhythm, 40
Classmates, 11
Clinical Psychological Science, 40
Clinton, Bill, 22
Common Sense Media, 76, 78–79, 99, 105–106
Community Memory, 10–11
confidentiality, 14–15
    See also Internet privacy; personal

information
conflict resolution, 66–67
Congress, 24
content filters, 38
Cook, Tim, 94, 106
cookies, 20–21, 45–46, 55–56, 58
    See also targeted advertising
creativity, 32, 80
crime, 87, 91
cyberbullying, 18–19, 26–29, 35–38, 73–74, 79, 101, 103
cyberstalking, 38, 74, 95–96

Daboll, Peter, 59, 104
depression, 18, 29, 39–40
digital footprint, 19, 23–24, 41–42, 61–62, 88–96
direct messages (DMs), 75
discrimination, 59–60, 75, 98
distraction, 69–71, 78
doxing, 82, 90
drug abuse, 39

education, 12, 32, 35–36
Electronic Privacy Information Center, 22, 99
email, 10, 75, 84–85
emotional support, 28, 32–33, 77–80
    See also friendship
empathy, 30
employment, 39, 42, 71, 80, 87, 91
European Union, 22

Facebook
    addiction to, 66
    communication via, 7, 12, 15
    discriminatory advertising on, 59–61, 104
    and law enforcement, 95, 106
    location services on, 91
    Mark Zuckerberg and, 20, 24
    as news source, 94
    and privacy concerns, 83–84, 92
    privacy settings and, 23–24
    private profiles on, 93
    and procrastination link, 70, 105
    statistics on, 27
    and targeted advertising, 47–48
facial recognition technology, 24
Fair Housing Act, 60–61

INDEX

AUTHOR'S BIOGRAPHY AND CREDITS

ABOUT THE AUTHOR

Ashley Nicole is an author and true crime writer with a background in psychology and sociology. Though a California native, she currently lives in Arizona, where she enjoys hiding from the sun and writing novels.

PICTURE CREDITS